Old LANGHOLM and the]

by
Alex F. Young

Langholm High Street, from the Buck Hotel to the Town Hall, as it was in 1895.

Standing on Watchknowe, above Langholm's Skipper's Bridge, the Round House was built as a summer house by George Maxwell of Broomholm in 1833. In this photograph from the early twentieth century it has an air of abandonment, but worse was to come when the roof was lost to vandalism. The structure still stands, but the door and a window on the far side have been stoned up.

Text © Alex F. Young, 2003.
First published in the United Kingdom, 2003,
by Stenlake Publishing,
Telephone / Fax: 01290 551122

ISBN 1 84033 237 9

FURTHER READING

The books listed below were used by the author during his research. Only one title listed is available from Stenlake Publishing. Those interested in finding out more are advised to contact their local bookshop or reference library.

The New Statistical Account of Scotland, Vol. IV, Dumfries, Kirkcudbright and Wigtown, William Blackwood & Sons, 1845.

Dr Dorothy H. Booth, *Echoes From the Border Hills*, The Pentland Press, 1992.

John R. Hume, *Dumfries and Galloway: An Illustrated Architectural Guide*, The Rutland Press, 2000.

A.J. Mullay, *Rails Across the Border – The story of Anglo–Scottish Railways*, Patrick Stephens Ltd, 1990.

Gordon Stansfield, *Dumfries & Galloway's Lost Railways*, Stenlake Publishing, 1998.

John Thomas, *Regional History of the Railways of Great Britain, Volume 6 (Scotland): The Lowlands and the Borders*, David & Charles, 1971.

ACKNOWLEDGEMENTS

The author would like to thank the following for their assistance during his research: Marion Poole, Norman Gormley, Beryl Bailey, David Latimer, John Murray, Mrs Molly Murray, Stephen Laverack, Avril Grieve, Mrs Janet Armstrong, Ralph Mitchell, Anne Wightman, Arthur Tolson, Graham Greer, May Greer, Fiona McDonald, Lynda Whitford, Moira Johnstone, Lesley Knowles, Douglas Elliot, George Irving, John Riddick, Denholm Reid, Graham Bartlett of the National Meteorological Library, Bracknell, and Ruth Airley and Neil Moffat of the Ewart Library, Dumfries. The publishers wish to thank Ian McDowell for contributing the photographs on pages 9 and 40.

The view of Langholm from Heathery Hill, 1900. Deriving its name from the long stretch of 'holm' or flat land along the banks of the River Esk, Langholm's recorded history goes back to the Battle of Arkinholm, fought on 1 May 1455, when an army composed of leading Border families defeated the army of three brothers of the ninth Earl of Douglas, a victory which marked the end of the Black Douglases. At this time the parish – there would have been no town as such – was known as Staplegorton. When the Earl of Nithsdale granted it baronial burgh status in 1610, it won the right to hold fairs and markets, but not the right to foreign trade which was reserved for towns with royal burgh status. It was also made a burgh of regality for the Duchess of Buccleuch in 1687. In 1703 it became a parish and in 1743, by disjoining the five parishes of Eskdale from Middlebie and those of Castleton from Jedburgh, a presbytery was formed.

The coming of the Industrial Revolution in the late eighteenth century brought change, through industrialisation, to the quiet market town and development at New Langholm across the river began to appear to house the new workers in cotton manufacture. By the end of that century the River Esk was powering 3,552 mule spindles. Initially, only ninety to a hundred people were employed, but the number grew with the increasing range of products produced – woollen yarns, stockings, stuffs, serges and plaids. In his *Topographical Dictionary of Scotland* from the 1840s, Samuel Lewis wrote of New Langholm that it '[adjoins] the town of Langholm and, containing 1,057 inhabitants, this village . . . was erected by the Duke of Buccleuch in 1778 . . . and consists of about 140 houses, constructed in a regular plan . . . each with a portion of land.' By the end of the nineteenth century the Langholm tweeds of Reid & Taylor and Arthur Bell were widely recognised and today the town has the headquarters of the Edinburgh Woollen Mill chain. This picture shows Langholm's Market Place and Town Hall on a late afternoon in the days before the First World War. Built in 1811, possibly by the Kelso architect William Elliot, the Town Hall stands on the site of its seventeenth century predecessor.

Apart from cotton manufacture, Langholm's other industries, albeit small, included brewing, distilling and tanning. In July 1864, to open up new markets and bring in raw materials for these industries, the Border Union Railway arrived on a single track line from Riddings Junction on the 'Waverley Line'. The service ultimately lasted some thirty days short of a full century. Although Langholm was a staging post on the Carlisle to Edinburgh road from early times, later improvements to the A7 trunk route helped to alleviate the loss of the railway. Enterprise and initiative have eased the town's transition into its post textile period and today there is increased tourism and a diversity of local employment ranging through ceramic modelling, leather tanning, specialist textile design, contract weaving and internet website provision. This view is of Market Square and High Street in the early 1930s; since then little, other than trading names, seems to have changed. John Hume sold hats and hosiery, while Malcolm's shop, previously owned by John J. Thomson and later by Errington and Murray, was a licensed grocer.

This photograph of Langholm Post Office from around 1902 also gives a glimpse of the Square and High Street on the left and the warehouse, remembered as the workshop of the mason Thomas Telfer, to the right. As a boy, the poet Hugh McDiarmid is said to have worked in the post office (his father was a local postman). MacDiarmid – real name Christopher Murray Grieve – was born in Langholm in 1892 and became the greatest figure in twentieth century Scottish literature, being particularly famous for his epic poem 'A Drunk Man Looks at the Thistle'. A founding member of the National Party of Scotland (predecessor of the Scottish National Party), he was also a Communist and enjoyed the distinction of being expelled from both parties. He remained active in literature and politics until his death in 1978.

Eskdale Temperance Hotel, Langholm.
Headquarters of the Celebrated Eskdale and Liddesdale
Coaching Tours. (Wm. Douglas, Proprietor.)

The Eskdale Temperance Hotel in Market Place was built as the King's Arms Inn by William Elphinstone in 1866. By the time of this photograph from around 1908, it was owned by William Douglas. One of the property's surviving deeds is entitled 'Instrument of sasine in favour of William Armstrong, writer in Langholm. In all and whole the tenement of houses and yeard [sic] within mentioned. 28 June 1796.' As the Eskdale Hotel, it still welcomes visitors to the town.

A detachment of local recruits to the King's Own Scottish Borderers are cheered along High Street, past the Crown Hotel, on their way to the First World War. How many of their names are now on the obelisk in Buccleuch Park? The Crown Hotel started as a staging post and only in the early nineteenth century did it become a three storey building. To its left is the present Royal Bank of Scotland building, built in 1864 by the National Bank of Scotland (this was taken over by the Royal Bank in 1969).

The Thomas Hope Hospital for the Poor, photographed in 1910. When ten year old Thomas Hope left Langholm with his mother in 1819 to join his father in America, he could not have imagined how munificent his return would be some seventy years later. The family prospered, building a chain of thirty grocery stores in the area of New York. On a visit to Langholm in the summer of 1888 (by no means his first), Thomas arranged that on his death an endowment would provide a hospital for the poor in the community. He died on his birthday – 3 March – two years later and on 21 September 1896 his sister, Jane Hope, laid the memorial stone of the building. It officially opened on 28 May 1898, but the fact that the first patient was not admitted until the following December must say something about the health of Langholm folk.

Branching off the main, forty-three mile long, Hawick to Carlisle line at Riddings Junction, the first train into Langholm arrived on 29 March 1864, carrying parts for the turntable which terminated the seven mile single track branch. At one time up to 350 passengers were using the thirty-two services which were provided each week. The site of the station buildings has now been taken by a car park, where a stone cairn commemorates the departure of the last train on 15 June 1964.

Langholm Academy, on Thomas Telford Road, in the spring of 1905 when Mr John Howie (died 1908) was rector over some 600 pupils. He had been appointed in March 1876 when the School Board (formed on 8 April 1873 under the Education (Scotland) Act of 1872) brought together pupils from a number of independent schools into the Parish School which was renamed Langholm Academy. The necessary extension, to accommodate the 570 pupils and staff of six certificated teachers and eleven pupil teachers, can be seen in the centre and to the left. In 1962 this building became Langholm Primary School when the academy moved to new premises opposite.

Of the 600 Langholm men who volunteered for service in the First World War – joining regiments such as the KOSB, the Royal Scots Fusiliers, the HLI and the Black Watch, and serving in campaigns ranging through France and Belgium, Gallipoli, Egypt, Palestine, Africa, Italy, Russia, Salonica, and at sea – 130 of them gave their lives. The seven foot Angel of Victory and Peace, which stands atop a thirteen foot high Cornish granite base, was unveiled in Buccleuch Park by the Duke of Buccleuch on Wednesday, 27 July 1921. A press report gives the memorial's cost as £1,300 and in Provost James Cairns's speech there was a hint of difficulty at the committee stage: 'In selecting the memorial it was impossible to please all tastes,' he said, 'Criticisms have been carefully considered and it is now hoped that approval will be generous and criticism gentle.' The fountain to the right in the photograph was presented by Provost Cairns in 1925, but was vandalised and later removed.

Two flocks of sheep on their way to market one early Monday morning in 1921. Taken from the Buck Hotel, the photograph shows John Murray the postman (known as 'Jock the Post'), dressed in 'civvies', coming across the right-hand side of the bridge as Will Scott and his dog Jyp from Burnfoot Farm in the Ewes Valley follow the sheep. The flock would have overnighted in a field close to town, having been driven the eight miles from the valley the previous day. On the right of the group in the foreground is Andrew Elliot of Mosspeeble Farm in the Ewes Valley, while leaning on his stick is Jimmy Elliot from Burnfoot Farm.

Built in the late 1860s by the woollen manufacturer John Scott (1838–1894), Ashley Bank became a hotel in the mid-1920s when it was bought by Mrs Barbara Younger. This photograph dates from her time. On her death in 1945, the business was carried on by her daughters, Charlotte and Janet, for a further four years until they sold to William and Charlotte Lunn, who continued the business. If the gardens reflect the accommodation, it must have been a comfortable hotel. Ironically, in the late 1980s ownership of the house almost came full circle when it was bought by the Edinburgh Woollen Mill.

Photographed during a rehearsal break, at the rear of the buildings behind George Street and John Street, Langholm Amateur Dramatic Society pose in costume for their production of *Jeanie Deans*, which they staged in the Buccleuch Hall on 13 and 14 March 1906. The cast included the Misses Belle M. Waldie and L. Scott (the female leads), May Waldie, J. Taylor, M Taylor and J. Hyslop (as Geordie Robertson and the Duke of Argyll respectively), G. Hyslop, R.E. Morrison, J.D.M. Copland (as Dumbiedykes), M. Beattie, J.J. Elliot, H. Conacher, W. Allison, W. Johnstone, G. Herries, H. Gavin and H. Calvert. In this picture, so far only local builder John Hyslop (centre front row, with the beard), 'who spent more time entertaining than building' and who died in the late 1940s, and his brother Gavin Hyslop (died 1955; fifth from right, front row) have been identified. The *Eskdale and Liddesdale Advertiser* reported on a well staged production under the management of the well known Glasgow actor, Mr John Clyde. Rarely performed today, the music for this 'grand opera' was composed in 1894 by Hamish MacCunn (1868–1916) for the Royal Carl Rosa Opera Company. The question of a dramatic society producing an opera was put to rights in 1923 with the founding of Langholm Amateur Operatic and Dramatic Society which is still going strong. Their first production was Gilbert and Sullivan's *Mikado*.

Photographed by local master photographer Simon Carruthers in front of New Langholm Bowling Club's 1898 pavilion (built when their old venue gave way to the hospital), children from the academy pose in highland dress during what must have been an entertainment staged by the school. Working in Langholm, Carruthers (born in 1849) was the son of Charles, a watchmaker, and Catherine Carruthers of No. 17 David Street. His brother Charles followed their father in the family business.

Another group of school children, again photographed by Carruthers, dressed for a production of the *Mikado*.

Langholm.

A 1920s view of Langholm from Watchknowe, where it can be seen that for a short stretch the River Esk, the road and the railway followed parallel tracks.

This time the camera has moved onto Hall Path, bringing the railway station just in on the left and Ashley Bank on the right. Just left of centre of the picture are the gas works and its chimney.

Framed here by Skipper's Bridge, Langholm Distillery has stood on the banks of the River Esk since 1765. Taking water from a spring on Whita Hill and grain from the surrounding fields, the distillery was hit by poor harvests in the 1790s and converted to a paper mill. Using cotton and flax fibre, its twenty workers could produce eighty reams (500 sheets) per week, each ream selling at twenty shillings. Paper production ceased around 1812 and by 1815 whisky was again being produced. In 1917 the old problem of grain shortage arose again and put an end to distillation. The building lay empty until bought by the Tolson family, from Ossett in Yorkshire, in 1927. After much demolition and rebuilding, it is still home to the family and the Border Esk Filling Station and Garage. Skipper's Bridge was built in 1690 and commemorates a retired sea captain who at one time ferried people across the river.

Common Ridings are a Borders' tradition and in Langholm's case it dates to a land settlement case in the Court of Session at Edinburgh in 1795, from which came the annual event of marking out the town's boundaries. This photograph is of the Common Riding of 1910. Although the day started with a slight frost, this was to be the wettest of Riding Days. Here, with the banner Provost Easton had put into his trust for the day, is Cornet Arthur Irving, accompanied by his predecessors, James J. Paterson (cornet of 1909) and James Young (cornet of 1908). Already umbrellas are in evidence and by the afternoon even the wrestlers were tardy in coming into the ring. The suggestion of hiring a hall for the evening dance was dismissed, the crowd now being so wet. When Cornet Irving returned the flag the Provost thanked him for carrying out his duties despite the weather.

The oldest surviving brass band in Scotland, Langholm Brass Band is reputed to have played the Royal Scots Greys through the town on their return from the Battle of Waterloo in 1815. The silver buckle present to them that day is preserved in the Town Hall. In 1964 they participated in the UK Brass Band Championship, held that year in Hammersmith Town Hall, and when Sir Christopher Collett, who had a holiday home near Langholm, was elected Lord Mayor of London in 1988 the band was invited to take part in the parade.

It is not known when the local Flute Band was founded, but since 1862 they have been playing their part in the Common Riding Day by rousing the town from its slumbers at 5.00 a.m. Indeed, it is now the only day of the year when they come together.

The girls of the town parading with their heather besoms, which, along with the Barley Bannock and the Salted Herring to symbolise thirlage and fishing rights, are paraded with the Spade, used to dig the boundary ditches, and the Scotch Thistle and the Floral Crown. They are crossing the temporary bridge from the Kilngreen back to town on Common Riding Day. One of the marquees on the green has a sign board saying 'Mrs A. Watt, Douglas Hotel'. The 1881 census shows the Douglas Hotel at No. 86 High Street with thirty-seven year old Adam Watt as hotel keeper, living with his wife Jane, aged thirty-three, their three children, Adam (six), Jane Ann (three) and Isabella Hill Watt (one). Their two servants, twenty-one year old Jessie Scott from Tundergath and sixteen year old Katherine Hannah Whitelaw, are also recorded. This photograph cannot be dated accurately but it would appear that Jane Watt was by then a widow.

'They're off!' Dating from 1845, the first event of the Common Riding Day, starting at 6.30 a.m., is the hound trail (organised according to the rules of the Northern Counties Hound Trailing Association), with spectators often organising 'sweeps' on the race. This photograph of the starting line at Collin's Turn shows the hounds just before the 'off'. Ahead of them is a ten mile circuit which, on a good day, will take twenty-five minutes. The first dog over the finish line wins its owner the cup and a prize, which at the time of this photograph, *c.*1910, would have been around £4.10/-. Afterwards all adjourned to town for a breakfast of 'barley bannock and saut herrin', a tradition which still continues.

This photograph from around 1904 shows the sports field on Castle Holm. Sports events on the Common Riding Day have included, as can be seen here, wrestling, as well as stone wrestling (under the rules of the Cumberland and Westmorland Wrestling Association), the standing high leap, the running high leap, the pole leap and foot races.

Craigcleugh, Langholm

Off the Westerkirk road out of Langholm, this 1896 photograph shows Craigcleuch House and the valley known as the 'Gates of Eden', just over twenty years after the house was built by the woollen mill owner, Alexander Reid. Sadly he did not live to see it completed and it was sold to General Sir John Ewart, on whose death in 1906 it passed to his son, General Sir Spencer Ewart, who was General Officer Commander in Chief for Scotland at the outbreak of the First World War. The ghosts which haunt the house are said to have the power to unbolt and unlock doors.

Ewes Post Office and Telegraph Office (and later telephone exchange), *c*.1906. When Brieryshaw Cottage became the post office is not known, but that the Ewart family ran it from the beginning is not in dispute. The left end of the building was a blacksmith's shop, with the yard to the rear, where William Ewart worked until his death in 1912 at the age of sixty-nine years. His son, also called William, followed him in the smiddy, while his daughter-in-law, Isabella, ran the post office. Unusually they did not sell provisions, only cigarettes. Isabella died in 1949 aged seventy, and William the following year at the age of sixty-nine. The post office business passed to their daughter Minnie, who late in life had married George Slack, a retired farmer remembered as 'George o' the smiddy'. When the area telephone exchange was installed in the post office, Minnie, as the operator, could always be relied upon to 'know what was happening'. On her retirement in the mid-1970s, the post office closed. The building had the misfortune to stand on the verge of the A7 trunk route and was demolished in the early 1990s during a road improvement scheme.

Just over six miles south of Langholm, Canonbie had quite a different history to its larger neighbour. As suggested by the root of its name, 'the residence of the Canons', the village's early history lies with the church and the lands of Canonbie Priory were confirmed to the Augustines of Jedburgh in 1165 by King William the Lion. Following the Battle of Solway Moss on 24 November 1542, the priory was sacked and the lands later fell to the Duke of Buccleuch who became the sole proprietor. On its way to Langholm, the Industrial Revolution by-passed Canonbie and it remained a agricultural community, although in the eighteenth century there was coal mining at nearby Rowanburn. Today the village serves as a dormitory for Carlisle which is just seventeen miles to the south. This 1930s view of the village, photographed from the High Road, shows the Public Hall with the road sweeping right, passing Bowholm and the Riverside Hotel before crossing the bridge and making its way up the Cut towards Rowanburn and Newcastleton.

'In all the glory of a beautiful autumn afternoon' (as reported by the *Eskdale and Liddesdale Advertiser*), the Duke of Buccleuch addresses the assemblage at the unveiling of Canonbie's war memorial, erected on the garden ground of Miss Lockie, on Sunday, 23 September 1921. The forty-seven names on the memorial include Adam Routledge, the nineteen year old grandson of Mr A. Routledge of Blinkbonny, Canonbie, who was a private with the Machine Gun Corps and who died on 18 April 1918 and was buried at Zonnebeke, West Vlaanderen, Belgium; Lance Corporal Charles G. Craigie, twenty-six year old husband of Henrietta of No. 35 Rowanburn, who died on the first day of the Somme; and nineteen year old James J. Steele, a private with the Royal Scots, whose parents, Matthew and Jeanie Steele lived at No. 23 Rowanburn. He was killed on Wednesday, 16 October 1918.

A view from the 1930s showing 'Woodhouse', the post office premises, on the right and the Cross Keys Hotel on the bend beyond. At that time John Edgar ran the post office, while James Millar managed the hotel on behalf of a Glasgow based company.

Built as a coaching inn around 1660, the original Cross Keys building was at the near end of the white two storey row in the centre of the picture (where the public bar is now). This was extended in 1700 and by 1800 the building had taken the shape shown here and which we know today. At the time of this 1920s photograph, Annie Elder was innkeeper. The Cross Keys kept abreast of the times, abandoning the stables at the rear of the premises to build a garage on the roadside. Gordon Flitcroft is remembered running it, but following a fire in 1982 it closed.

Designed by the Langholm architect James Burnet, Canonbie Public Hall is seen here in the spring of 1913 just as the finishing touches were being added. The Duke of Buccleuch had gifted the site and £300 towards the final cost of £1,400 for the 400 seater, electrically-lit, hall. The balance was raised by public subscription and several bazaars. On Friday, 2 May 1913 the Earl of Dalkeith attended the opening ceremony which was followed by a concert and dance. The Earl handed over the feu charter for the site to Mr Lewis Beattie, the chairman of Canonbie Parish Council, and in return was presented with a silver key to mark the occasion. The hall is still the centre of village activities.

Canonbie Railway Station, photographed in 1921. This was the first station on the line to Langholm from Riddings Junction which branched off the Hawick to Carlisle line. It was named 'Canobie' when it opened in May 1862, but was renamed Canonbie on 1 February 1904. Along with the stations at Langholm, Glentarras and Gilnockie, it closed on 15 June 1964.

In this photograph Mr Robert Smellie stands at the 'Disruption Meeting Place' above the Hollows and there is now a commemorative plaque at the site which states: 'Canonbie United Free Church founded on this site 1843'. Through the 1830s the established church was riven by conflict over lay patronage in the appointment of ministers and the state's interference in church affairs. It resulted in the Disruption – the resignation of 470 of the Church of Scotland's 1,200 ministers and their congregations' subsequent attempts to re-establish themselves as the Free Church of Scotland. One difficulty, experienced not only in Canonbie, was in persuading the feudal landlord, in this case the Duke of Buccleuch, to grant them land on which to build new churches for themselves. Parliament became involved and eventually the Duke and other landowners were forced to relent. Canonbie's new Free Church was opened on the first Sabbath of 1851. Robert Smellie was born in Langholm in 1820 and for many years ran a drapery business in the High Street. Never married, he devoted his life to the community and the Free Church and was a trustee of the Thomas Hope Hospital. He died in March 1913 at the ripe old age of ninety-three.

In times past Road End was a major crossroads. In this view the road passing the front of the cottage has come up from Annan, via Canonbie and Rowanburn, on its way to Jedburgh (now the A6357), while the cottage gable on the left side faces onto the B6318 from Langholm as it heads south to Newcastle-upon-Tyne. Around the time of this photograph, c.1906, the house was rented from the Duke of Buccleuch (at nine pounds and ten shillings per annum) by John Armstrong, grocer. The children standing in the doorway may be his. Thomas Gass the blacksmith had his premises on the opposite corner of the junction.

The original Gilnockie, or Hollows, Tower, on the banks of the Esk, was built by the Armstrong family around 1518 and destroyed about ten years later. This tower, with a base measuring twenty-three by fifteen feet and a height of forty feet to the corbel, is of a later date. Some time after this early twentieth century photograph was taken the roof collapsed, but the building was later restored and made into a dwelling.

Opening in December 1864, Gilnockie was the last station on the Langholm branch to open. Canonbie had already been operating for over two years. This photograph from 1907 appears to show the stationmaster, who, according to the valuation roll, would have been John Hogarth. With the other stations on the branch, it closed on 15 June 1964.

With the Scottish coalfield running from Ayrshire to Fife, it is difficult to think of Dumfriesshire as a coal mining area. But as early as 1700 there were drift mines in the area and the *New Statistical Account* of 1836 reported collieries at Archerbeck and Byreburn. The village of Rowanburn owes its existence to coal as the Duke of Buccleuch opened the mine there, bringing in miners and their families between 1860 and 1863. With the community and its housing came the village store, photographed here in the early 1900s, with the colliery chimney, demolished in 1935, standing above it. Due to its relative isolation, its wide ranging stock included not only provisions, but hardware, clothing, calico, tartans, animal feed and lamp oil. Recently, a business scroll day book, kept by one-time owners Mr and Mrs Robert Easton Moffat, was found in a bricked up part of the premises. Typical of the five accounts recorded on 6 June 1913 is the following: 'Mr A. Fox, Canonbie Station, 1 stone of Potatoes – 9d, Bacon – 1/-, Bread – 6d, Butter – 11d, Oatmeal – 6d, Rice – 4d, Tea – 1/-.'

Rowanburn Colliery, photographed around 1908 with a line of North British Railway wagons waiting to be filled. Mining the rich seam of good quality coal became uneconomic in 1922 and the colliery was closed. A memorial wheel was erected to commemorate both the mine and Samuel Lindsay, who was killed by a tub falling on an incline a mere six months before closure.

Ten Row (there being ten houses in the row) was part of the original village built in the 1860s to accommodate mining families; another row was Barrel Row, so called because each house had a rainwater barrel by the front door. Piped water was only installed in 1958/59. By then the mining families had either moved on or passed on, but as part of a modernisation programme the streets of the village were tarmacked. In December 2002 a planning application to build fifteen houses in the village was passed.

The Loaning at Bentpath, from the hill to the south-west, in the early 1920s. In the lower right corner is the Bentpath Hotel (at one time known as the Flying Spur public house) which closed around this time. From there the road leads through the hamlet and across the bridge to Westerkirk Parish Church which was rebuilt on an ancient site in 1880. The bridge was built in 1756 and gave access to an antimony mine in the hills beyond. Ivy Cottage, in the bottom left, was home for many years to Robert Law the tailor.

Bentpath in the early 1930s, looking from the bridge to the main road. Law the tailor's cottage is on the right, with the village hall beyond it. Built in 1921 for use by ex-servicemen, it was a school for evacuees in the Second World War and became the village hall in 1948. The five cottages on the left – one of which was Bentpath Post Office, then run by Miss Graham – were auctioned in 1912 at the break-up of Westerhall Estate.

Viewed across a field of corn stooks on Richard Johnstone's Bentpath Farm are Westerkirk Parish Library, on the left, and the parish school. In 1793 a collection of books was amassed for employees of the Westerhall Mining Company which was at that time extracting antimony (which was alloyed with lead to increase its hardness) from a mine in the hills above. At the closure of the mine in 1798, the books were transferred to the school. At his death in 1834 the civil engineer Thomas Telford, who was born on nearby Glendinning Farm in 1757, left a bequest for the creation of a library and in 1852 these premises were put up at a public subscription cost of £600. The school closed in 2000 and its five remaining pupils were transferred to Langholm Primary. Telford, one of the greatest civil engineers of the nineteeth century, was responsible for the building of the Menai Suspension Bridge and St Catherine's Dock in London, as well the Caledonian Canal.

The cottage at Allangillfoot, eight miles north of Langholm on the Eskdalemuir road, pictured around 1900 with Margaret Jardine, granddaughter of the occupant, John Jardine, standing at the doorway. Jardine, an agricultural labourer, had rented the house from local landowner, Richard Bell, since the 1870s. The 1881 census describes him as a fifty-six year old from St Mungo, Dumfriesshire, living with his wife Margaret, their five children and two granddaughters, seven year old Margaret and ten month old Janet. The Elliot family and their two children also lived in the house. Old John died unexpectedly in June 1906, aged eighty-one years, and when Janet called Dr Thorburn from Hartmanor House (built in the early 1880s), he certified that death was due to natural causes. In 1947 the cottage was purchased by the Forestry Commission, but it is now privately owned.

Eskdalemuir's Holm School, named after Holm Farm which stands just out of picture to the left, photographed around 1900. The Rev. William Brown, writing in the *New Statistical Account* in the 1830s, speaks of one private school and one parochial school. The latter may have been in what later became the head teacher's house, pictured on the right. The school building on the left was erected in 1872 and its records for 1897 shows the following entries: '28 May – six children (due to sale at Cote Farm); 22 June – closed for Jubilee Holiday; 24 June – closed early for summer through lack of attendance; 18 December – eighteen boys and nine girls.' It was also noted that on the latter date an inspector visited the school and reported that Mr Malcolm (presumably the teacher) '[was] doing admirable work in this small school . . . the general intelligence of all the classes, the excellence of the penmanship and the accuracy of the arithmetic all deserve special commendation.' It was also reported that Standard Five had mastered fractions and proportions, Standard Four were working on the multiplication of money, while Standard Three were working on simple multiplication. Today, the school has a role of just six pupils.

Although Davington is an ancient settlement, said to have been named after King David I (1084–1153), it was virtually abandoned by 1900 and only with the coming of the Observatory in 1906 did it gain a new lease of life. Stretching out across this view, with the Observatory behind, are the manse, the village school and the parish church.

At the close of the nineteenth century radiation from London's expanding electric railway system had rendered magnetic meteorological observations at Kew Observatory worthless, so the search began for a site that was radiation free for a ten mile radius. By moving a proportionately sized coin over a map of Britain, Eskdalemuir was decided upon. According to the *Eskdale and Liddesdale Advertiser*, the site, on Nether Cassock Farm, was visited by surveyors from Kew in May 1903 when, unusually, the weather was 'wet and stormy, and somewhat unfavourable to field work'. The first sod was cut at a ceremony on 19 July that year and by the spring of 1906 the contractors, Henderson & Duncan of Edinburgh, had progressed to the point shown in this photograph.